Dogbert and Dilbert appear regularly in their own comic strip, DILBERT™, made available to your hometown paper, college newspaper, or business newsletter by the fine folks at United Feature Syndicate.

CONTENTS

FOREWORD by Dogbert

Many pompous business books have been written in the last few years. This is another one. But unlike its predecessors, this book offers practical information.

Other business books have offered such useful insights as "profitable companies pay high salaries." What exactly are we supposed to do with that kind of information? Should unprofitable companies raise salaries to become more profitable?

Let's face it, companies that are profitable are usually in the right place at the right time, and that's all there is to it. Those companies could be managed by gerbils and they would still make money hand over paw. Sure, in the beginning somebody invented something valuable, or stole it from somebody else, but since then it's been strictly auto-pilot.

So forget about making the company more profitable; it's out of your control. Put your energy where it will make the most difference: surviving your frustrating and thankless job.

What the world needs is a <u>practical</u> guide to business—one which the average white collar worker can understand and use. That's why I wrote **Dogbert's Big Book of Business**. That's why it has simple cartoon pictures.

To research this book I spent nearly two weeks working at a large American company. This was long enough to become an expert by American standards, but not so long that the life force would be sucked out of me.

I hope you enjoy my book.

DRESSING FOR SUCCESS

MEN'S BUSINESS CLOTHES

WOMEN'S BUSINESS CLOTHES

WOMEN UNDERSTAND HOW TO USE BUSINESS CLOTHES TO CONVEY SUBTLE MESSAGES.

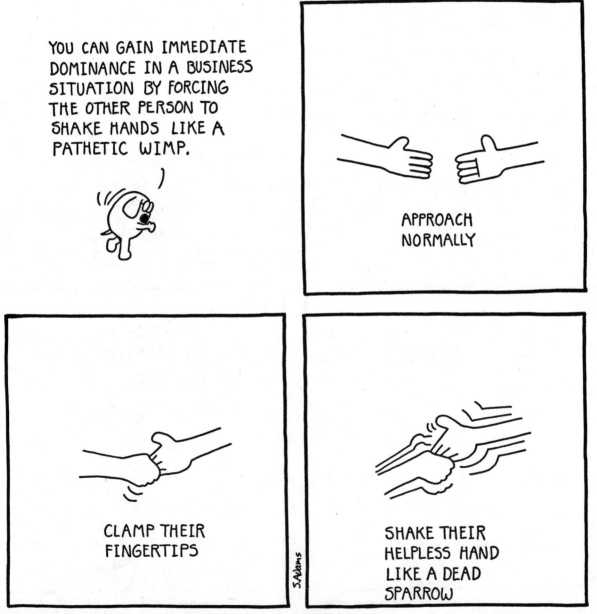

HALLWAY ETIQUETTE

THE ACCEPTED RULES OF HALLWAY ETIQUETTE COVER ONLY THE FIRST TWO TIMES YOU RUN INTO THE SAME PERSON IN THE SAME DAY. AFTER THAT, YOU MUST IMPROVISE.

SALARY ETIQUETTE

IT IS CONSIDERED IMPOLITE TO ASK CO-WORKERS THEIR SALARIES; HOWEVER, IT IS PERFECTLY ACCEPTABLE TO DEDUCE IT BY GRILLING THEM RELENTLESSLY ON THEIR SPENDING HABITS.

DOGBERT'S LEISURE PERCEPTION PRINCIPLE

THE DOGBERT HARP

IF SOMEBODY MISSPEAKS AT A MEETING, IT IS YOUR OBLIGATION TO HARP ON IT OVER AND OVER AGAIN.

...AND GROSS SALES ARE DOWN TEN PERCENT THIS MONTH.

YOU MEAN YEAR, NOT MONTH.

TEN PERCENT THIS MONTH?!! IT'S IMPOSSIBLE. YOU HAVE LOST ALL CREDIBILITY. HOW CAN WE TRUST ANYTHING YOU SAY?!!

I MEANT "YEAR"... I MISSPOKE.

TEN PERCENT A MONTH?!! DO YOU TAKE US FOR IDIOTS?!!

PERSONAL PHONE CALLS

IF YOU HAVE A PERSONAL LIFE, LET
EVERYBODY ENJOY IT. SIGNAL YOUR
CO-WORKERS TO LISTEN TO YOUR
PERSONAL CALLS BY CHANGING YOUR
POSTURE AND LOWERING YOUR VOICE.

OFFICE POLITICS

DEMAGOGUERY

DOGBERT'S LAUGHTER GUIDE

THE AMOUNT OF ENERGY SPENT LAUGHING AT A JOKE SHOULD BE DIRECTLY PROPORTIONAL TO THE HIERARCHICAL STATUS OF THE JOKE TELLER.

LAUGHING AT YOUR BOSS'S JOKE

HEE HEE! I'LL HAVE TO REMEMBER THAT.

YOUR BOSS'S BOSS'S JOKE.

HA HA HA !! I'LL HAVE TO WRITE THAT ONE DOWN.

YOUR BOSS'S BOSS'S BOSS'S JOKE

HA HA HA

I'LL HAVE TO TATTOO THAT ON MY BACK !!!

STAYING OUT OF TROUBLE

IT IS BETTER FOR YOUR CAREER TO DO NOTHING, THAN TO DO SOMETHING AND ATTRACT CRITICISM.

OFFICE POLITICS

YOUR BOSS REACHED HIS/HER POSITION BY BEING POLITIC-ALLY ASTUTE. DON'T TURN YOUR BACK.

TAKING CREDIT FOR OTHER PEOPLE'S WORK

IT IS MUCH EASIER TO TAKE CREDIT FOR OTHER PEOPLE'S WORK THAN TO DO YOUR OWN. GRAB EVERY OPPORTUNITY TO ASSOCIATE YOURSELF WITH PROJECTS WHICH ARE ALREADY SUCCESSFUL.

I AGREE WITH EVERYTHING YOU'RE SAYING HERE, SO PUT ME DOWN AS CO-AUTHOR.

I CAN DROP THAT REPORT OFF WITH THE BOSS FOR YOU.

WHY DON'T WE JUST ADD YOUR REPORT TO THIS COVER PAGE I CREATED ALL BY MY-SELF.

S.Adams

DE-POLITICIZING YOUR BUSINESS WRITING

BE CAREFUL THAT WHAT YOU WRITE DOES NOT OFFEND ANYBODY OR CAUSE PROBLEMS WITHIN THE COMPANY. THE SAFEST APPROACH IS TO REMOVE ALL USEFUL INFORMATION.

TAKE OUT THE DISCUSSION OF THE PROBLEM; IT COULD EMBARRASS SOMEBODY.

AND DON'T MENTION THE ALTERNATIVES; IT WILL JUST RAISE QUESTIONS.

OKAY, WHAT'S LEFT?

THE PAGE NUMBERS.

INEFFICIENCY AND YOUR CAREER

YOUR CAREER DEPENDS ON HOW MANY PEOPLE WORK UNDER YOU. IT IS IN YOUR BEST INTEREST TO INVOLVE AS MANY PEOPLE AS POSSIBLE IN ANY TASK. THAT WAY YOU CAN JUSTIFY INCREASING YOUR STAFF.

KISSING UP

IF YOU HAVE NO SPECIAL
TALENTS, AN UNGLAMOROUS
METHOD IS AVAILABLE TO
DISTINGUISH YOURSELF IN
YOUR BOSS'S EYES.

I THINK YOU COULD
ALL TAKE A LESSON
IN CORPORATE RESPECT
FROM WHAT'S-HIS-FACE
HERE.

CHANGE FOR THE SAKE OF PROMOTION

YOU WILL APPEAR TO BE A VISIONARY PLANNER IF YOU DECENTRALIZE EVERYTHING WHICH IS CENTRALIZED AND CENTRALIZE EVERYTHING WHICH IS DECENTRALIZED.

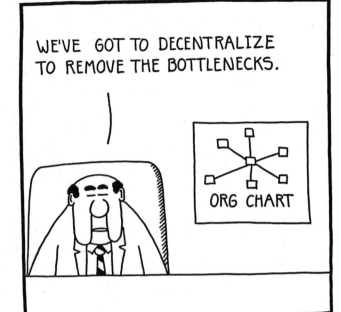

INSENSITIVITY: YOUR KEY TO MANAGEMENT SUCCESS

MONEY

CHANGES TO THE SALARY PLAN

ANY CHANGE TO THE SALARY PLAN WILL
RESULT IN LESS MONEY FOR YOU. IF
THEY WANTED TO GIVE YOU <u>MORE</u> MONEY,
THEY WOULDN'T HAVE TO GO THROUGH
ALL THE TROUBLE OF CHANGING THE PLAN.

THIS YEAR, ALL
RAISES WILL BE
ROUNDED TO THE
NEAREST TEN
PERCENT.

YOURS ROUNDS
DOWN TO ZERO.

YOUR SALARY

EVERY NIGHT, AFTER THE EMPLOYEES LEAVE, THE EXECUTIVES GET TOGETHER TO LAUGH ABOUT YOUR SALARIES.

WHAT MOTIVATES MANAGERS

MONEY AS A MOTIVATOR...

HERE'S YOUR RAISE.

POINK

COMPANIES WITH NO MEANINGFUL MANAGEMENT INCENTIVES OF THEIR OWN END UP BEING MANAGED BY AIRLINE BONUS MILES PROGRAMS

PRIDE AS A MOTIVATOR...

HERE ARE YOUR NEW BUSINESS CARDS. THEY SPELLED YOUR NAME WRONG BUT I FIGURED IT DIDN'T MATTER.

BONUS MILES AS A MOTIVATOR...

THE STAFF MEETING WILL BE IN AUSTRIA THIS WEEK!

I'LL BE THERE!

FANTASY BUDGETING

PLANNING YOUR BUDGET

THERE IS NO RELATIONSHIP
BETWEEN YOUR ASSESSMENT
OF YOUR BUDGET NEEDS AND
WHAT YOU ACTUALLY RECEIVE.

THE GOOD MANAGEMENT PENALTY

MANAGEMENT SALARY INCENTIVES

THE BUREAUCRACY

GROUP WRITING

DOGBERT'S THEORY OF EMPLOYEE SUGGESTIONS

KNOWING THE ENEMY

BEFORE YOU CAN DEFEAT THE COMPETITION, FIRST YOU MUST DEFEAT YOUR OWN COMPANY.

THIS IS THE PROJECT PLAN...

WE'LL IGNORE OUR LEGAL DEPARTMENT...

BYPASS THE ACCOUNTING DEPARTMENT...

INSTIGATE A FIGHT BETWEEN MARKETING AND OPERATIONS...

AND PRAY NOBODY NOTICES OUR PROJECT.

S.Adams

THE DOGBERT SHUFFLE

YOUR PERCEIVED VALUE TO THE COMPANY IS DIRECTLY RELATED TO THE VOLUME OF PAPER YOU SHUFFLE. REQUEST COPIES OF ALL DOCUMENTS, NO MATTER HOW UNRELATED TO YOUR RESPONSIBILITIES.

DID YOU READ THE NEWSPAPER TODAY?

NO. CAN YOU MAKE A COPY FOR ME?

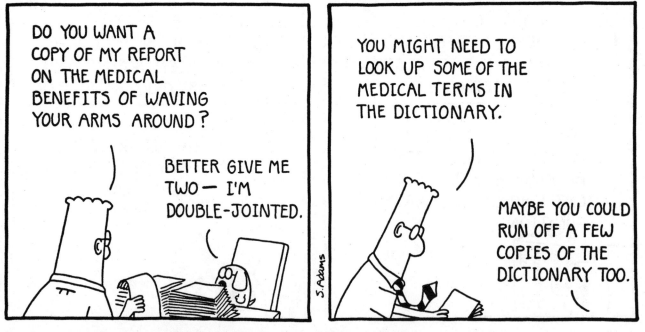

DO YOU WANT A COPY OF MY REPORT ON THE MEDICAL BENEFITS OF WAVING YOUR ARMS AROUND?

BETTER GIVE ME TWO — I'M DOUBLE-JOINTED.

YOU MIGHT NEED TO LOOK UP SOME OF THE MEDICAL TERMS IN THE DICTIONARY.

MAYBE YOU COULD RUN OFF A FEW COPIES OF THE DICTIONARY TOO.

MAKING EXCEPTIONS

EXCEPTIONS MUST NEVER BE MADE; THEY ONLY LEAD TO WIDESPREAD EFFICIENCY AND A DIMINISHED NEED FOR PEOPLE IN YOUR JOB.

NO

I'M REQUESTING SEVEN DOLLARS FOR MY RESEARCH PROJECT.

WHAT? THERE'S NO COST-BENEFIT ANALYSIS ... NO EXTENSIVE DISCUSSION OF ALTERNATIVES... NO FINANCIAL ANALYSIS ...

THAT WOULD TAKE MONTHS, AND I'D HAVE TO MAKE UP MOST OF THE NUMBERS ...

IF YOU FOLLOW PROCEDURES, I WON'T HAVE TO RISK MAKING A DUMB DECISION.

DOGBERT'S LAW OF BUREAUCRATIC GRIDLOCK

BUREAUCRATIC GRIDLOCK IS CAUSED BY PEOPLE WITH DIFFERENT PRIORITIES WHO PRACTICE GOOD TIME MANAGEMENT.

DID YOU GET THE INFORMATION I NEED FOR MY IMPORTANT PROJECT?

NO. IT'S NOT IN MY TOP THOUSAND PRIORITIES.

DID YOU BRING THE INFORMATION I REQUESTED FOR MY IMPORTANT PROJECT.

NO, BECAUSE YOUR PROJECT DOESN'T MATTER TO ME.

THOSE TIME MANAGEMENT CLASSES SURE HAVE FREED UP OUR SCHEDULES.

THE ANSWER DEPENDS ON THE ASKER

NEVER ANSWER A QUESTION UNLESS YOU KNOW EXACTLY WHO IS ASKING, WHY IT IS BEING ASKED, AND WHAT WILL BE DONE WITH THE INFORMATION.

THE ADVANTAGE OF SMALL COMPANIES

BIG COMPANIES USE MOST OF THEIR RESOURCES TRYING TO KEEP PEOPLE FROM GETTING MAD AT THEM. SMALL COMPANIES HAVE MORE FLEXIBILITY.

THE BENEFITS OF TITLE INFLATION

INFLATED JOB TITLES IN MIDDLE MANAGEMENT ALLOW THOSE AT THE BOTTOM OF THE COMPANY HIERARCHY TO AVOID TRULY DEMEANING TITLES.

VICE PRESIDENT

ASSISTANT VICE PRESIDENT

EXECUTIVE MANAGER

MANAGER

PEON

ASSISTANT PEON

TEMP

BOOT-LICKING, LOWER-THAN-DIRT, ASSISTANT PEON.

S.Adams

PERFORMANCE AND PRODUCTIVITY

COFFEE PERFORMANCE GUIDE

YOUR HAPPINESS AND JOB PERFORMANCE ARE INFLUENCED MORE BY COFFEE THAN BY ANY OTHER FACTOR.

NO COFFEE

ONE CUP

TWO CUPS

THREE CUPS

FOUR CUPS

CUBICLES

CONTRARY TO ANY COMMON SENSE NOTIONS YOU MIGHT HAVE, SCIENTISTS HAVE PROVEN THAT EMPLOYEES ARE HAPPIER AND MORE PRODUCTIVE IN CUBICLES THAN IN OFFICES.

I THINK I'D BE MORE PRODUCTIVE IN AN OFFICE INSTEAD OF THIS CUBICLE.

RIDICULOUS. SCIENTISTS HAVE PROVEN THAT PEOPLE LOVE CUBICLES.

HE FOUND THE CHEESE AGAIN.

HE LOVES IT IN THERE.

S. Adams

YOUR BOSS

LAW OF PROXIMITY

THE NEARER YOU ARE TO YOUR BOSS'S OFFICE, THE LOWER THE QUALITY OF YOUR ASSIGNMENTS.

BASIC MANAGEMENT TYPES

ALL MANAGERS FALL INTO ONE OF SEVERAL CATEGORIES. THE BEST YOU CAN HOPE IS TO HAVE A BOSS WHO DOESN'T NAUSEATE YOU OR KILL YOU.

TRADITIONAL

GET ME SOME COFFEE OR I'LL SLAY YOUR ENTIRE FAMILY.

SELF-DEPRECATING

I AM UNWORTHY TO BREATHE THE AIR YOU HAVE BURPED.

CHEERLEADER

OKAY EVERYBODY, LET'S FORM A HUMAN PYRAMID!!

MANAGEMENT STYLES (CONTINUED)

KEEPING THE BOSS INFORMED

BOSSES NEVER UNDERSTAND WHY THEIR STAFF IS RELUCTANT TO WARN THEM ABOUT PROBLEMS UNTIL IT'S TOO LATE.

THE PROJECT MIGHT NOT BE AS EASY AS WE HOPED.

WHAT?!!

YOU IDIOT!! I'LL FIRE YOU AND ANYBODY WHO LOOKS LIKE YOU!!

WHY DON'T THEY COME TO ME SOONER?

READING BODY LANGUAGE

PERFORMANCE APPRAISALS

IF A MIRACLE OCCURS AND YOUR BOSS ACTUALLY COMPLETES YOUR PERFORMANCE APPRAISAL, IT WILL BE HASTILY PREPARED, ANNOYINGLY VAGUE, AND AN INSULT TO WHATEVER DIGNITY YOU MIGHT STILL POSSESS.

CO-WORKERS

SUFFERING FOOLS

AS YOU SUSPECTED, ALL OF YOUR
CO-WORKERS ARE FOOLS. YOU MUST
LEARN TO PITY AND TOLERATE
THEM.

WAIT A MINUTE...
EVERYBODY HERE IS
A FOOL EXCEPT ME.

DATING CO-WORKERS

THE BOSS'S SECRETARY

THE MOST PERILOUS CHALLENGE YOU WILL EVER FACE IS DEALING WITH THE BOSS'S SECRETARY. IT MAY BE NECESSARY TO OFFER A LIVE CALF OR A SUMMER INTERN AS AN ANIMAL SACRIFICE.

I JUST NEED A FEW MINUTES ON THE BOSS'S CALENDAR.

FIRST, YOU MUST DEFEAT ME IN A BATTLE TO THE DEATH IN THE PIT OF THE FIRE-BREATHING LIZARDS.

UNDERSTANDING ACCOUNTING PEOPLE

PEOPLE WHO WORK IN ACCOUNTING DEPARTMENTS OFTEN WORK TWELVE-HOUR DAYS CREATING REPORTS THAT NOBODY CARES ABOUT. THIS GIVES THEM A VERY BAD ATTITUDE. DO NOT ATTEMPT HUMOR AROUND THEM.

ARE YOU THE CLERK WHO RETAINS ALL OF THE BUDGET ANALYSIS RECORDS?

WHAT IF I AM?

THEN I GUESS YOU COULD BE CONSIDERED "ANALYSIS RETENTIVE."

Hee Hee

HE WAS MIGHTY FAST WITH THOSE SCISSORS.

MARKETING

TRANSLATING MARKETING TALK

PEOPLE IN MARKETING JOBS ALWAYS SPEAK IN CODE.

OOWA OOWAGA

WE DID EXHAUSTIVE CUSTOMER RESEARCH.

MEANING: I ASKED MY CAT, MITTENS.

I'M SURE WE CAN SELL A MILLION UNITS.

MEANING: YEAH, RIGHT, WHEN PIGS FLOSS.

WE'RE WORKING CLOSELY WITH THE ENGINEERS.

MEANING: WE TOLD THEM OUR FAVORITE COLORS.

UNDERSTANDING MARKETING PEOPLE

PEOPLE ENTER THE MARKETING PROFESSION AFTER THEY REALIZE THAT THEY HAVE GROWN UP WITHOUT ANY PARTICULAR SKILLS.

I SAY WE SHOULD LISTEN TO THE CUSTOMERS AND GIVE THEM WHAT THEY WANT.

WHAT THEY WANT IS BETTER PRODUCTS FOR FREE.

OH... THEN LET'S JUST SELL THEM WHAT WE'VE GOT AND CALL IT A STRATEGY.

S. Adams

PERKS

BUSINESS LUNCHES

WHEN USING THE COMPANY'S MONEY
TO PAY FOR A MEAL, IT IS EXPECTED
THAT YOU WILL ORDER THE MOST
EXPENSIVE ITEMS ON THE MENU.

STEALING OFFICE SUPPLIES

SICK DAYS

SICK DAYS ARE THE SAME
AS VACATION DAYS, BUT
WITH SOUND EFFECTS.

THE JOY OF FEEDBACK

FEEDBACK IS A BUSINESS TERM WHICH REFERS TO THE JOY OF CRITICIZING OTHER PEOPLE'S WORK. THIS IS ONE OF THE FEW GENUINE PLEASURES OF THE JOB, AND YOU SHOULD MILK IT FOR ALL IT'S WORTH.

THANKS FOR REVIEWING MY REPORT.

IT'S GARBAGE.

I'LL SPRAY PAINT THE REALLY STUPID PARTS.

AND WHAT FLEA MARKET SOLD YOU THAT GOD-AWFUL DRESS?

LEGAL OWNERSHIP OF YOUR PEN ENDS WHEN YOU TAKE YOUR EYES OFF OF IT. YOUR CO-WORKERS ARE WAITING FOR ANY OPPORTUNITY TO MAKE IT THEIR OWN.

MEETINGS

USING STEREOTYPES TO SIZE UP A MEETING

YOU CAN USE STEREOTYPES TO RAPIDLY DETERMINE WHO HAS THE MOST POWER AT A BUSINESS MEETING.

RETURNING CALLS DURING A MEETING: MUST BE A MIDDLE MANAGER.

BROUGHT A BAG LUNCH: MUST BE A TECHNICAL PERSON.

HAS NO WRITING MATERIALS: MUST BE A SENIOR EXECUTIVE.

UNAWARE THAT VESTS ARE NOT IN STYLE: MUST BE A BUDGET ANALYST.

TOO MUCH MAKE-UP AND CLEAVAGE: SECRETARY WHO MAY BE HAVING AN AFFAIR WITH AN EXECUTIVE.

TRYING TO LOOK MORE RELAXED THAN ANYBODY ELSE: PROBABLY AN EXECUTIVE.

THE IMPORTANCE OF DONUTS

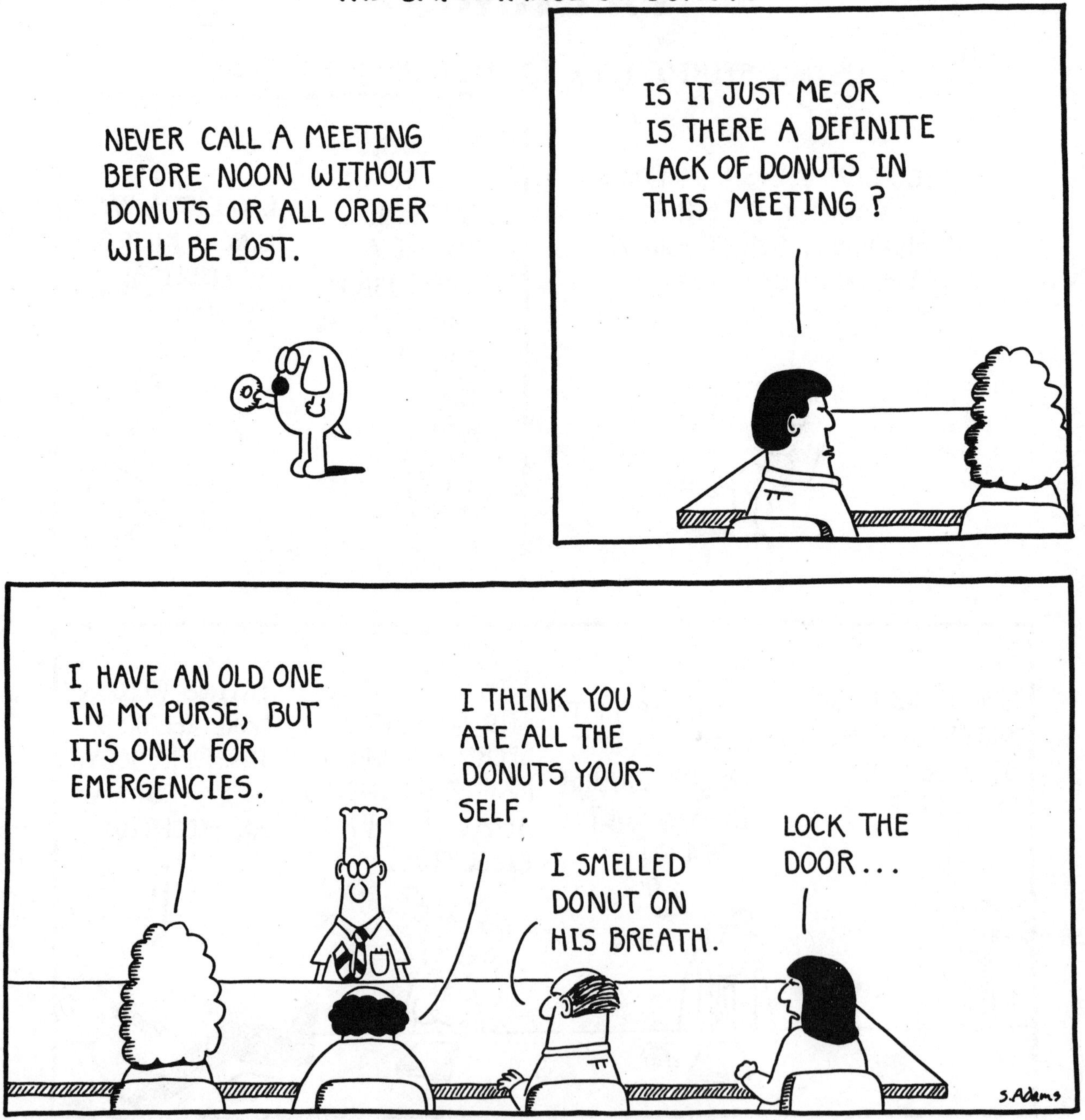

DOGBERT'S GROUP I.Q. FORMULA

THE INTELLIGENCE QUOTIENT OF ANY MEETING CAN BE DETERMINED BY STARTING WITH 100 AND SUBTRACTING 5 POINTS FOR EACH PARTICIPANT.

S.Adams

2 PEOPLE

WHAT DO YOU THINK?

THERE ARE MANY ISSUES...

3 PEOPLE

WHAT ARE THE ISSUES?

IS IT OUR MISSION TO THINK OF ISSUES?

THAT'S AN ISSUE.

4 PEOPLE

LET'S WRITE A PURPOSE STATEMENT.

THAT COULD BE OUR MISSION.

IS THAT LIKE AN OBJECTIVE?

THAT'S AN ISSUE.

DEALING WITH MEETING BOREDOM

YOU CAN ACTUALLY DIE FROM THE BOREDOM CAUSED BY LONG BUSINESS MEETINGS. THERE ARE THREE BASIC STRATEGIES FOR SURVIVAL:

FANTASIZE

CRACK JOKES

IS THAT YOUR NOSE OR DID A WEASEL CLIMB ON YOUR FACE AND DIE?

GO FOR IT

ZZZZZ

USING MEETINGS TO AVOID WORK

ATTENDING MEETINGS IS CONSIDERED "WORKING" EVEN IF YOU DON'T DO ANYTHING BUT SIT THERE. TRY TO ATTEND AS MANY MEETINGS AS POSSIBLE.

CAN YOU HELP ON MY PROJECT TODAY?

TODAY? NO, I'VE GOT A MEETING OF THE KELP SUPPORT TEAM THIS MORNING...

THEN A MEETING OF MY YOUNG CANINE CLUB...

THEN MY TASK FORCE ON PRODUCTIVITY...

DOGBERT'S RULE OF THREE

NOTHING PRODUCTIVE EVER HAPPENS
WITH MORE THAN THREE PEOPLE IN
A ROOM, BECAUSE SOMEBODY IS
ALWAYS TOO DISTRACTED TO
PARTICIPATE IN A MEANINGFUL WAY.

FRIDAY AFTERNOON MEETINGS

CALENDAR MULTIPLIER EFFECT

IT IS FUTILE TO TRY TO ARRANGE A MEETING WITH MORE THAN THREE PARTICIPANTS. BEYOND THREE IT IS STATISTICALLY IMPOSSIBLE TO FIND A DATE WHEN ALL OF YOU WILL BE AVAILABLE.

THE FIRST TIME EVERYBODY ELSE IS AVAILABLE IS JUNE 8TH IN THE YEAR 3057...

WELL, YEAH, I SUPPOSE YOU WILL BE DEAD BY THEN...

SO I GUESS YOU'LL BE FREE THAT WHOLE DAY.

S. Adams

THE DILBERT DRONE

THE MOST EFFECTIVE WAY TO RESPOND TO A QUESTION IS TO DRONE ENDLESSLY ABOUT UNRELATED TOPICS. THIS HAS THE DUAL ADVANTAGE OF AVOIDING GIVING WRONG ANSWERS AND REDUCING THE VOLUME OF FUTURE QUESTIONS.

WEASEL WORDS, BLUFFING, AND LYING

WEASEL WORDS

WEASEL WORDS ARE WORDS THAT ARE TRUE WITHOUT BEING INFORMATIVE. THEY ARE USEFUL IN SITUATIONS WHERE A CLEAR EXPLANATION WOULD BE EMBARRASSING.

HOW DO I SAY THE PROJECT FAILED BECAUSE THE PROJECT MANAGER IS AN IDIOT?

WHAT DID YOU MEAN WHEN YOU SAID I HAVE A "GENETIC PREDISPOSITION TOWARD SUB-OPTIMAL PERFORMANCE"?

IT MEANS IT'S NOT YOUR FAULT.

THE VALUE OF BUZZWORDS

BUZZWORDS ARE VALUABLE FOR INTIMIDATING OUTSIDERS AND MAKING THEM THINK YOU'RE SMARTER THAN YOU REALLY ARE.

DOGBERT

I'M WANTING A JOB.

WE'VE PROACTIVELY PRIORITIZED OUR QUALITY MISSION OBJECTIVES AND REACHED A BREAKTHROUGH STRATEGIC CONCENSUS THAT OUR BOTTOM LINE WOULD BE NEGATIVELY IMPACTED BY THAT PATH FORWARD.

YEAH, AND WE DON'T HIRE PEOPLE WHO TALK FUNNY.

DOGBERT'S RULE OF BUSINESS LIES

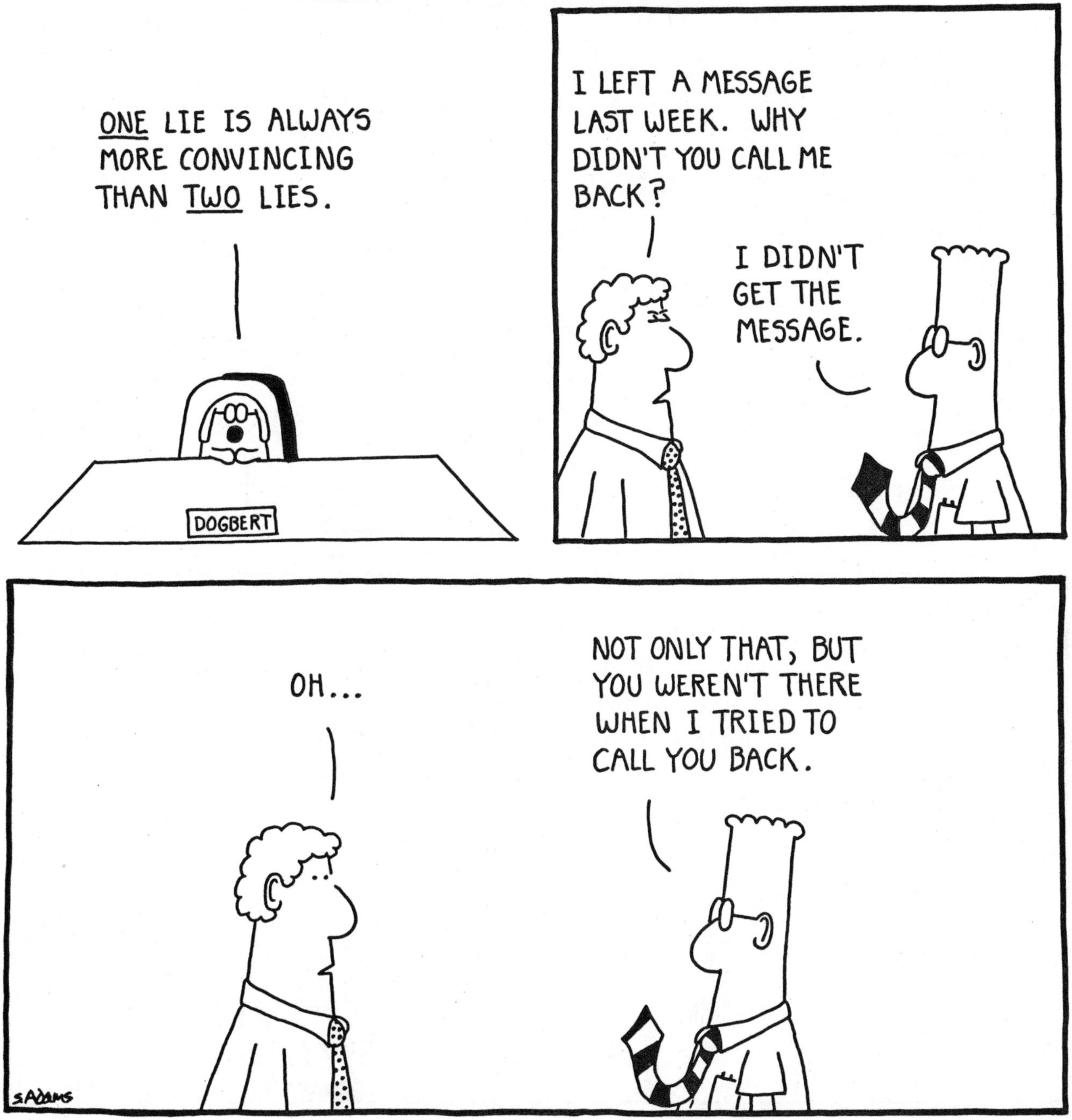

LYING ON YOUR RÉSUMÉ

NOBODY EVER GOT A JOB BY BEING COMPLETELY HONEST ON THEIR RÉSUMÉ. MAKE YOUR LIES BOLD, CREATIVE, AND ABOVE ALL: UNVERIFIABLE.

YOUR RÉSUMÉ SHOWS TWENTY YEARS AS A SENIOR EXECUTIVE AT THE CIA...

YES, AND THEY ARE INSTRUCTED TO KILL ANYBODY WHO TRIES TO CHECK ON IT.

EXCUSES FOR BEING LATE

NOBODY GOES TO MEETINGS ON TIME AND NEITHER SHOULD YOU. JUST REMEMBER THAT YOUR EXCUSE MUST BE MORE DRAMATIC THAN THOSE WHO ARRIVE BEFORE YOU.

YOU'RE LATE.

TRAFFIC WAS TERRIBLE. I THINK THERE WAS AN ACCIDENT.

I WAS THE ACCIDENT. I RAN OVER SOME KIND OF BIG ANIMAL.

SOMEBODY RAN OVER MY MOTHER.

TECHNOLOGY AND INNOVATION

INNOVATION

COMPANIES ARE GENERALLY SLOW TO ADOPT NEW WAYS OF BUSINESS, ESPECIALLY IF IT MEANS A REDUCTION IN THEIR BELOVED PAPER.

HOW TECHNOLOGY FREES US FROM WORK

TELECOMMUTE YOUR WAY TO MORE LEISURE TIME

FOR ONE BRIEF TECHNOLOGICAL WINDOW
IN HISTORY, IT IS POSSIBLE TO CLAIM
YOU ARE WORKING AT HOME BUT NEARLY
IMPOSSIBLE FOR YOUR BOSS TO CHECK ON
YOU. YOU SHOULD ARRANGE FOR AT LEAST
ONE TELECOMMUTE DAY PER WEEK.

NEXT ON OPRAH:
WORKERS WHO GET
PAID FOR STAYING
HOME DOING NOTHING.

s.Adams

LIE TO YOUR COMPUTER

COMPUTERS HATE PEOPLE. THEY WILL DESTROY YOUR DATA JUST TO BE MEAN. YOUR BEST STRATEGY IS TO LIE TO YOUR COMPUTER AND CONVINCE IT THAT YOU DON'T CARE ABOUT YOUR DATA.

ALL PROGRESS IS BASED ON FAULTY ASSUMPTIONS

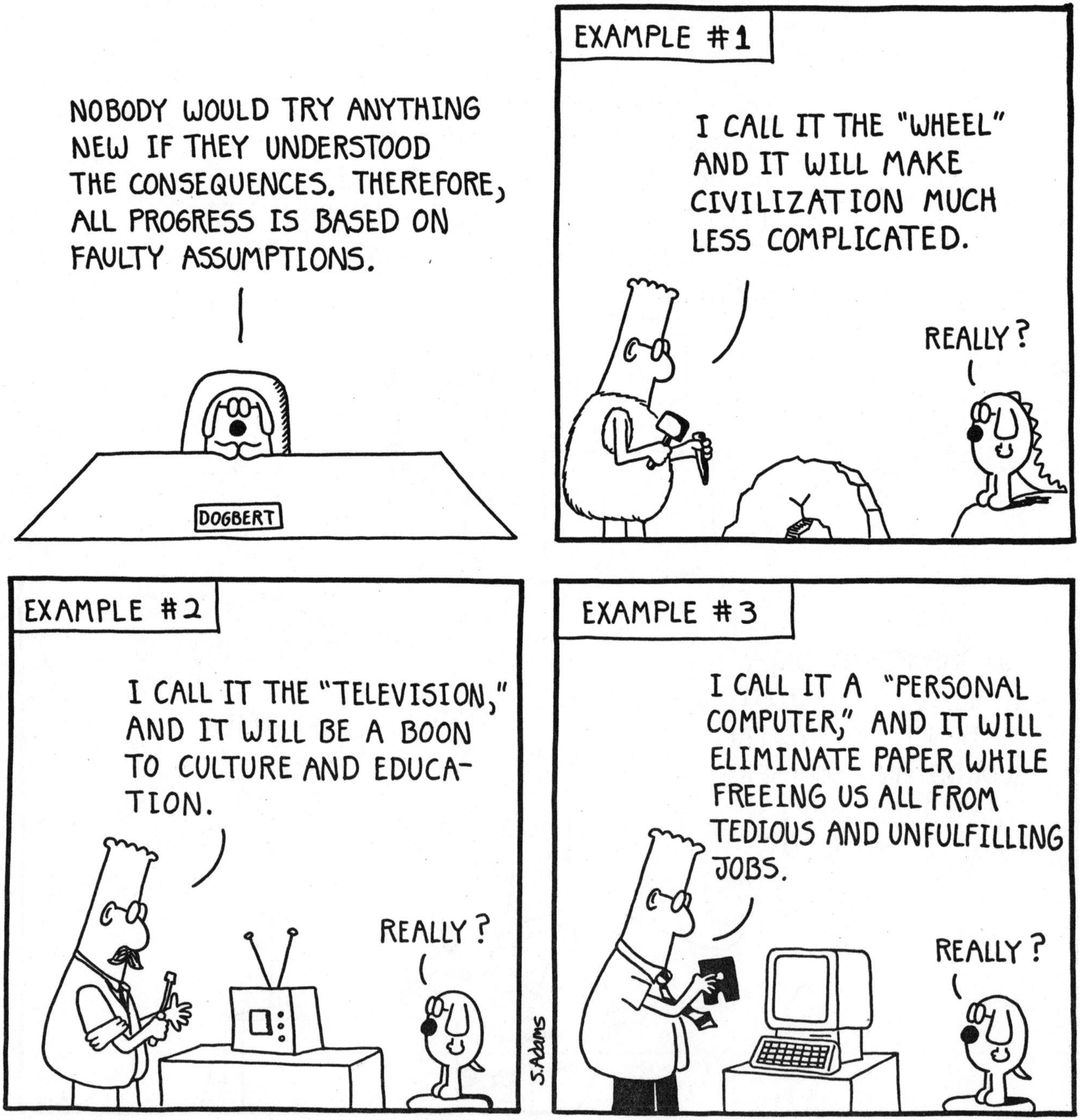

STYLE VERSUS SUBSTANCE

GREAT IDEAS CAN BE WRITTEN ON GARBAGE

THROUGHOUT HISTORY, MANY GREAT IDEAS STARTED AS SCRIBBLES ON THE BACKS OF ENVELOPES, MATCH BOOKS, AND COCKTAIL NAPKINS. BUT UNLESS YOU'RE PRETTY CONFIDENT ABOUT YOUR IDEA IT IS BEST TO USE REGULAR PAPER WHEN YOU SHOW IT TO THE BOSS.

THIS IS IT? THIS IS YOUR PROPOSAL?

YES SIR, WRITTEN ON THE CORN FLAKES I WAS HAVING WHEN THE IDEA CAME TO ME.

I PROBABLY SHOULDN'T HAVE STAPLED THE PAGES TOGETHER.

THE POWER OF FORMATTING

A WELL-FORMATTED, STUPID PROPOSAL WILL GET FARTHER THAN A GOOD IDEA WHICH IS POORLY FORMATTED.

AT FIRST, I THOUGHT YOUR PROPOSAL WAS RIDICULOUS...

THEN I NOTICED HOW WELL-FORMATTED IT IS, YOUR CREATIVE USE OF ITALICS, THE HIGH QUALITY OF THE PLASTIC COVER... I MUST SAY IT SWAYED ME.

WAIT... WHAT'S THIS LITTLE TWO-DOTTED THING?

IT'S A COLON, SIR. THEY'RE ALL THE RAGE.

S. Adams

ANALYSIS AS A TOOL TO AVOID DECISIONS

THE DOGBERT DEFLECTION

WHEN ASKED A QUESTION, NEVER ADMIT THAT YOU DON'T HAVE THE ANSWER. INSTEAD, RESPOND WITH AN IMPOSSIBLE QUESTION OF YOUR OWN.

AVOIDING CRITICISM

THE BEST WAY TO AVOID CRITICISM IS TO ESTABLISH A REPUTATION FOR BEING IRRATIONAL AND BELLIGERENT AT THE SLIGHTEST EXCUSE.

YOUR REPORT IS ALMOST PERFECT.

ALMOST ??!

YOU'RE PREDJUDICED AGAINST DOGS, YOU BIGOT!! I KNOW YOUR TYPE... ALL SMILES, BUT SECRETLY A DOG HATER. I'VE GOT A LAWYER!!

OKAY, IT'S PERFECT, EXTRAORDINARY, INCREDIBLE.

REALLY, OR ARE YOU JUST SAYING THAT?

GETTING FIRED

BIG COMPANIES HAVE PROCEDURES THAT MAKE IT NEARLY IMPOSSIBLE TO FIRE ANYBODY. IF YOU HAVE NO CAREER AMBITION AND NO PRIDE YOU CAN TAKE GREAT ADVANTAGE OF THIS SITUATION.

WAAA- WAAA THWPHTH !!

I'M WARNING YOU, JOHNSON! ONE MORE WEEK OF THIS AND I'M GOING TO START THE DISCIPLINARY PROCESS !!

PRIORITIZING YOUR WORK

YOU CAN TELL HOW IMPORTANT AN ASSIGNMENT IS BY HOW IT IS COMMUNICATED TO YOU.

IN BASKET:
TOTALLY UNIMPORTANT. YOU MAY SAFELY IGNORE IT FOREVER.

TELEPHONE:
IGNORE IT. NO IMPORTANT ASSIGNMENT HAS EVER BEEN GIVEN OVER THE TELEPHONE.

RRRRING

PERSONAL THREAT:
MAKE SOME TIME ON YOUR CALENDAR.

TUESDAY?

THE IMPORTANCE OF STRATEGIES

ALL COMPANIES NEED A STRATEGY SO THE EMPLOYEES WILL KNOW WHAT THEY DON'T DO.

PESSIMISM AND JOB EXPERIENCE

AN OPTIMIST IS SIMPLY A PESSIMIST WITH NO JOB EXPERIENCE. PESSIMISM INCREASES STEADILY OVER A CAREER UNTIL THE TENTH YEAR AND THEN REMAINS CONSTANT.

JUST HIRED

GREAT IDEA! LET'S START RIGHT AWAY!

FIVE YEARS EXPERIENCE

WE TRIED THAT IDEA FIVE YEARS AGO. IT DIDN'T WORK THEN AND IT WON'T WORK NOW.

TEN YEARS EXPERIENCE

WE'RE ALL GOING TO DIE ... DIE OR GO TO JAIL ... IT'S THE END OF LIFE AS WE KNOW IT ...

S. ADAMS

THE RIGHT APPROACH

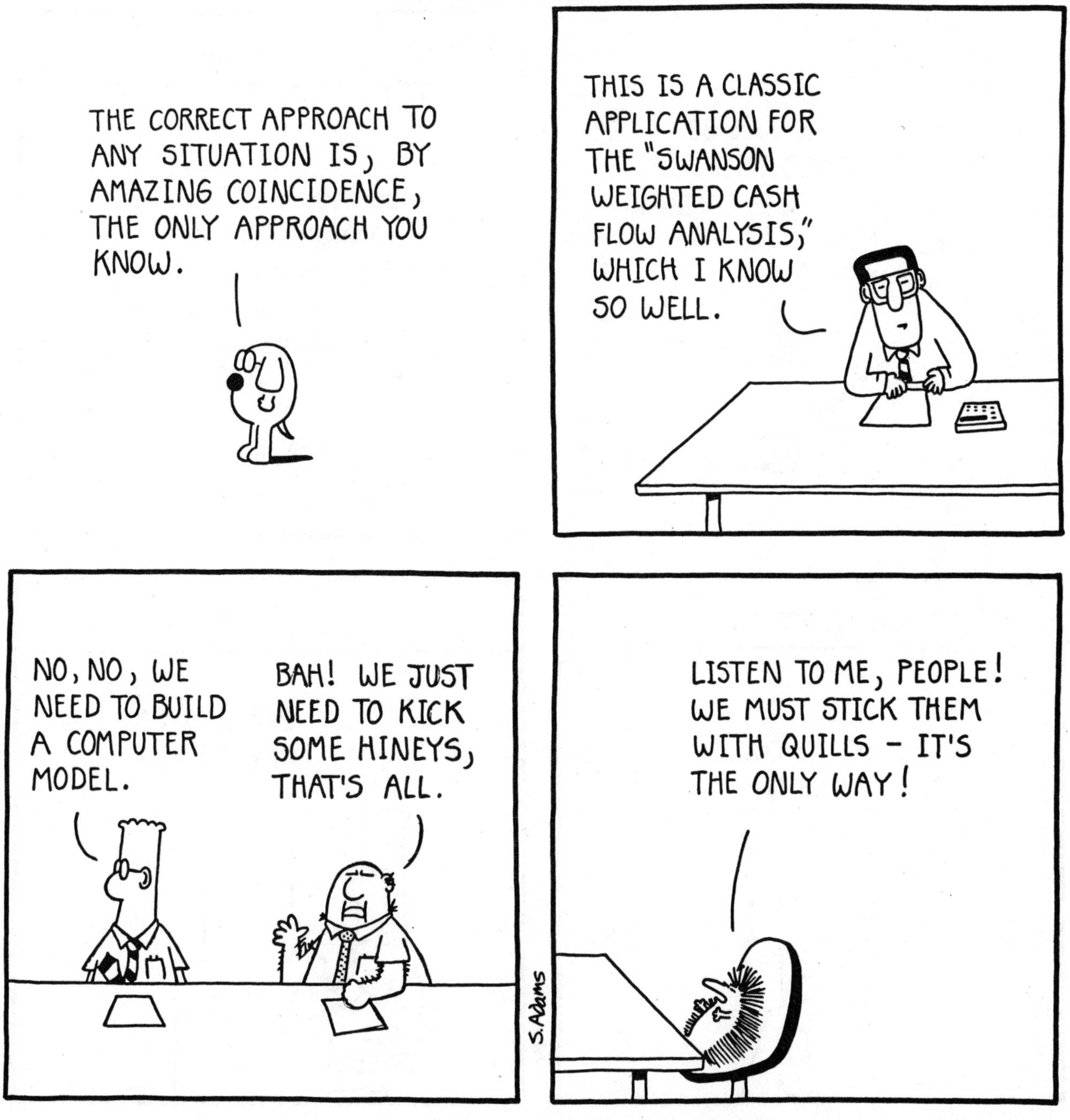

RUMORS

ALL RUMORS ARE TRUE — ESPECIALLY IF YOUR BOSS DENIES THEM.

I HEARD THAT WE'RE ALL GOING TO BE RECLASSIFIED AS "SERFS."

AND THEY'LL MAKE US WEAR PAPER HATS.

...AND WE'LL HAVE TO SALUTE ANYBODY FROM THE MARKETING DEPARTMENT!

THE LOBOTOMIES ARE SCHEDULED FOR TUESDAY!

THESE RUMORS ARE RIDICULOUS. WE ARE NOT CONSIDERING LOBOTOMIES...

CERTAINLY NOT AT THE PRICES WE WERE QUOTED.

DOGBERT'S RULE OF STRATEGIES

WHAT YOU DO

HOW TO IDENTIFY AN EXPERT

AN EXPERT IS A PERSON WHO HAS BEEN ASSIGNED TO AN EXPERT'S JOB. NO OTHER QUALIFICATIONS ARE NECESSARY.

WHEN TO CHANGE JOBS

CHANGING JOBS IS A TRAUMATIC AND DEGRADING PROCESS. YOU SHOULD ONLY DO IT WHEN YOUR CURRENT JOB BECOMES UNBEARABLE. FIND YOURSELF ON THIS GUIDE TO HELP YOUR DECISION.

KEEPING YOUR PERSPECTIVE

YOUR JOB IS UTTERLY INSIGNIF-
ICANT. BUT ON THE PLUS SIDE,
NOTHING YOU COULD DO WOULD
SERIOUSLY DAMAGE THE PLANET.
DON'T TAKE ANY OF IT TOO
SERIOUSLY.

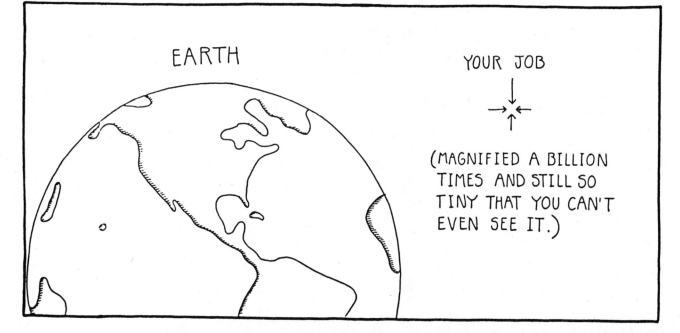

EARTH

YOUR JOB

(MAGNIFIED A BILLION
TIMES AND STILL SO
TINY THAT YOU CAN'T
EVEN SEE IT.)